Benin

Kit Elliott

Drawings by Gareth Floyd

GENERAL EDITOR TREVOR CAIRNS

CAMBRIDGE
AT THE UNIVERSITY PRESS 1973

front cover: The present Oba of Benin with two chiefs of the city. They are about to begin a ceremony in which the Oba pays homage to his father, his ancestors and all the dead of the nation. The Oba wears the state regalia with helmet, collar and corselet of linked coral beads. His armbands are of carved ivory. Although Benin city today is very different to the city the Portuguese saw in 1472, the Oba still performs some of the ancient ceremonies.

back cover: A pair of leopards made in the nineteenth century as copies of earlier examples. The leopards are $32\frac{3}{4}$ and 32 in (83 and 81 cm) high and each is carved from five separate elephant tusks. The 'spots' are formed from copper discs. In Benin the leopard was the main symbol of chieftainship because it stood for courage, strength, ferocity and cunning. You can see other examples of leopard symbolism in the bronze castings later in the book.

Published by the Syndics of the Cambridge University Press
Bentley House, 200 Euston Road, London, NW1 2DB
American Branch: 32 East 57th Street, New York, N.Y.10022

© Cambridge University Press 1973

ISBN 0 521 08028 2

Photoset and printed in Malta by St Paul's Press Ltd

The author and the publisher gratefully acknowledge the gracious permission given by Her Majesty the Queen to show the ivory leopards on the back cover of this book.

Thanks are also due to the following for permission to reproduce illustrations in this book:
Elizabeth McClelland, front cover and pp.17 (pottery), 30, 31, 32; Jack Barker and The United Africa Company Limited, pp. 5, 8, 9 (canoe with woman), 12, 13 (market), 17 (women with yams), 19, 47 (manillas); Bibliothèque Nationale, Paris, p. 7; Eastern Nigeria Information Service, p.9 (canoe with passengers); Adrian du Plessis, pp.13 (street scene), 15, 48; The Trustees of the British Museum, pp. 20, 21, 22, 23, 24, 25, 26, 27, 34, 36, 37, 39, 41, 42, 43, 45, 46, 47 (salt cellar); Cambridge University Library, p. 33; Radio Times Hulton Picture Library, p. 35; William Fagg, p. 38.

Contents

Introduction

This book is about a kingdom in West Africa as it was when Europeans saw it for the first time.

Already it had a long history. When reading about European voyages of discovery, we sometimes forget that the arrival of a few pale-skinned strangers may not have meant much to the people being 'discovered'. It has been easy for much more important events than this to vanish from the history of places like Benin, where the Africans had no writing. Information about the past was kept, of course, but in other ways. Officials in the royal court learned by heart what was important to the king and to themselves, and these facts might be handed on for hundreds of years. Ordinary people told stories of the past. But many things were left out, or changed, or just forgotten.

Europeans who came to Benin sometimes wrote about it. However, they seldom spoke the language and so they often misunderstood what they saw. Besides, they liked to tell a good story so they made the most of anything sensational, violent or weird. We have to make allowances when reading their accounts.

Fortunately, the studies of modern anthropologists often help us to make sense of the tales told by travellers or by the people themselves, though we cannot be quite sure how ideas and meanings may have changed during five centuries. Archaeologists, too, have begun to study what is left of old Benin, and have described its houses and walls, its tools and weapons, its ornaments and its graves.

So, though much remains uncertain, we can now make some attempt to understand. On the evidence we have at present, this is how it may have been in Benin five hundred years ago.

1. The end of a journey

Five hundred years ago a group of men put out in canoes from the banks of the Benin River. The mud-walled huts behind them were like any other African village on that part of the West African coast, where the River Niger divides into hundreds of waterways, and is lost among hundreds of square miles of marsh and forest as it flows into the Atlantic. The men in the canoes seemed unusually wealthy and well-dressed for such an ordinary place. Though they were naked to the waist, richly embroidered cotton kilts came down below their knees. They all wore strange round helmets, apparently made of leather or basketwork, with a curved rim, and flaps covering their ears. Around their throats were necklaces of red coral beads. One of the men seemed to be particularly important. His helmet was more elaborate than the others. A heavy rope of coral hung from his neck and lay upon his chest. From his waist were hanging little brooches and plaques of carved ivory and carefully worked bronze. There were bronze anklets on his legs, and bangles on his arms. He carried a wooden staff, white because the bark had been peeled off it. He spoke abruptly to the men who paddled the canoes, who were much poorer, wore no ornaments, and appeared to be rather afraid of him.

Out in the creek a small sailing ship lay at anchor in the rain. Its thread-bare sails hung limply from the yards. Water dripped on the soaking decks. The paintwork was worn. The crew were sick and miserable. Several had died. More were dying. One in three of the sailors would be dead before the ship returned to Portugal. It was, for them, a hateful coast. For 300 miles they had worked their way along the lagoons

A creek in the Niger delta. The mangrove trees stand with their huge roots reaching down into the mud. Much of the coast of what is now Nigeria is hidden by swamps like these. They made it very difficult for European sailors to go inland. It was not until 350 years after the Portuguese first saw these creeks that Europeans realised that the River Niger flowed through them into the Atlantic ocean.

and creeks which stretch from the country that was one day to be called Dahomey, along the coasts of what is now Nigeria. Far inland the black, brackish water wound among the gloomy mangrove trees. At low tide it ebbed past their shell-encrusted roots, and the mangroves stood in mile after mile of black mud. The mud stank. The rain fell endlessly. The only sound the sailors had heard for weeks had been that of the falling rain, the birds crying mournfully above their heads, and the insects whining and humming after dark. The sky was grey, the air hot, heavy and damp. The sails rotted; the ships' biscuit turned soft; and the clothes fell to pieces on their backs.

It was 1472 and Ruy de Sequira's ship had come to the end of its journey. It was the latest of many such ships that had set out down the West African coast since the beginning of the fifteenth century. Forty years before, an even smaller ship had set out from Portugal, and by rounding the dangerous shoals that stretched far out to sea from the desert Cape Bojador, and bringing a bunch of flowers to prove it, had shown that it was possible to sail down the coast of Africa and live. Since then other ships had sailed south from Portugal, each coming a little further than the last. By 1456 the first ships had passed the desert and Cape Verde had been named, the Green Cape where trees and grass grew south of the white sands of the Sahara. The first Europeans had reached the land of the Negroes.

The Portuguese had known little about Africa in those days, just as little as the Africans knew about them. The common sailors, at the beginning of the voyages, may have expected to find the water around the Equator boiling, or to return, if they returned, burned black as the Africans themselves. Even the men who had sent them – Prince Henry, the son of the Portuguese king, and later the merchant Fernao Gomes – had read the muddled reports in the old Roman geography books from travellers who may once have crossed the Sahara. They might not have been surprised if de Sequira had brought back news of: the catoblepas, whose heavy head was bent always toward the ground, fortunately for those who saw it, as one glance from its eyes would strike a man dead on the spot; the Blemmyae, who had eyes in their chests; the troglodytes, who lived in holes in the ground, spoke no language, and ate snakes.

Portuguese exploration on the West African coast

- - - - presumed route of de Sequira. Little known of voyage apart from arrival at or off Benin in 1472

///// Forest

×××× Southern limit of desert

Cape Bojador

Cape Verde

SONGHAI

R. Niger

MALI

KANEM

L.Chad

BENIN

Benin city

R. Benue

Gulf of Guinea

500 miles

500 kilometres

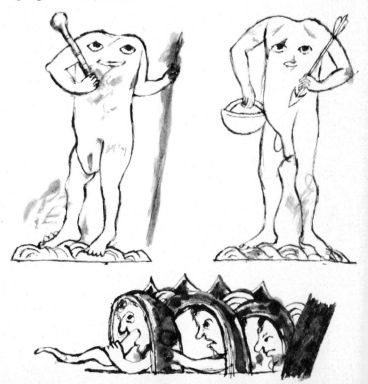

But what the Portuguese were to find was perhaps more surprising than all this.

As they waited on the deck of their ship for the canoes to reach them, the sailors must have wondered why they had accepted such discomfort, such a strong likelihood of death, so many months and so many thousands of miles from home.

The Portuguese had been looking for a kingdom. Prince Henry had known that it existed. It was called Mali, and it lay south of the Sahara. Its ruler, known as Mansa Musa, had been drawn on a map in 1375 by a Jewish mapmaker from Majorca, who had shown him sitting on a throne in the middle of the desert. He traded in gold.

Much of the gold in use in Europe at that time must have come originally from his kingdom, carried by camel caravan across the Sahara. To buy this gold the Portuguese had tried to reach Mali by sea, going behind their hated enemies, the Moors, who controlled the desert and its trade. But by the time a few Portuguese travellers reached Mali's capital, Mansa

This picture shows part of a map drawn by a Jewish mapmaker called Abraham Cresques, who lived in Majorca forty years before the Portuguese really started to explore the African coast. From North African traders he had learnt of the Negro king of the Mali empire. He shows him sitting on a throne with his crown, orb, and sceptre of gold. Towards him rides an Arab merchant. The names of the towns on the main trade route between Morocco and the River Niger are shown.

Musa had long been dead, and his empire was already disappearing, defeated by enemies from north and south. The other great Negro empires on the edge of the desert, Songhai and Kanem, were too far to the east for the Portuguese to reach. The Portuguese had at length found gold on the coast of what is now Ghana, where it was mined thirty or forty miles inland. They had even found a chief who used the same title as the emperor of Mali. He was Cara Mansa. His only empire was a few villages behind the sandy beach.

Canoes, big and little, on the Niger delta. The people of the creeks, who belong to the Ijaw and Itsekiri tribes, still live as much on the water as on land, while the people of Benin who come from further inland have as little to do with the creeks and canoes as they can. The simplest canoes are still hollowed out of a log; they are paddled from the stern, and may be helped along by a sail made of raffia.

Though this part of their quest had failed, the Portuguese were still searching for another kingdom, even more mysterious than Mali. For hundreds of years Europeans had believed in the land of Prester John, a Christian kingdom, ruled by a priest king who, before the world ended, would join with the Christians of Western Europe in one last holy war against the Muslims of North Africa and the East. For years the Portuguese had believed that such a kingdom lay in the depths of Africa. Ruy de Sequira, anchored in the Benin River, waiting for the canoes to reach him, may have believed himself nearer to the land of Prester John than any European so far.

The dignified men who were now about to come on board his ship probably knew more about his expedition than he could ever know about them and where they came from. Long before the Portuguese had arrived on the African coast, canoes had been making the journey through the lagoons and along to the coast where the gold was mined. For centuries they had been trading in slaves to work the mines, leopard and civet skins, the glands of the civet cat (which could be used for making perfume), blue cotton cloth, ivory, beads and kola nuts. (The kola nuts were chewed everywhere in West and

Left: Bigger canoes carry goods to market. Behind the woman who paddles her crops to be sold you can see yams, squashes, pumpkins and gourds. Bigger boats still, (like the ferry boat above), brought cargoes of salt, cloth, beads, ivory and slaves nearly 500 miles (800 km) through the creeks to trade with the people of what is now Ghana and Dahomey. The Portuguese took this trade over. By the end of the eighteenth century some of the largest canoes were armed with cannon to keep the European sailors from exploring too far up the creeks.

North Africa, just as Europeans were later to chew and smoke tobacco. They were welcomed by travellers for their bitter taste, after which even the foulest water tasted sweet.) During the last twenty years first rumours, then first-hand reports had been coming back of the arrival of the white men, of their desire to trade in gold, pepper or ivory, and of the slow progress of their ships eastward along the coast. The news of de Sequira's ship must have come weeks ahead of him from canoes slipping through the maze of waterways. Now royal officials were being paddled out to meet the first Europeans to reach their country. They were from a people called Edo. Their country was known to foreigners as Benin, and they were the representatives of the Oba, the king of Benin.

They climbed onto the deck of the little ship, and were given presents of trinkets and cloth by de Sequira. Then they too ordered that their own gifts of food and drink be unloaded, and gave permission to the Portuguese to land.

2. The road to Benin

There was nothing on the banks of the Benin River to show that de Sequira was on the frontier of a great kingdom. The Portuguese landed and, escorted by officials and porters, they were allowed to set off inland. The forest at once swallowed them up. Huge trees, teak and mahogany, towered a hundred feet above them, cutting off the light. A path wound in and out between the trunks. To leave it the travellers would have needed cutlasses to hack their way through the brushwood, thorn bushes and creepers that hemmed them in, snatched at their clothes, and prevented them seeing more than a few feet into the half light on either side of them. Had the pathway been left unused for a month the forest would have covered it entirely. Yet this was one of the main trading routes of Benin. From time to time columns of porters on their way to the coast, their heads heavily loaded with goods,

would see the white staff of the official at the head of the procession, and stand aside to let the travellers by. Everything had to be carried on men's heads in this forest. Horses and donkeys soon died from the tsetse fly and wheeled transport was unknown anywhere in tropical Africa.

Every two or three miles the track opened out into a village whose huts stood on either side. Nearby was an open space where there was often a market being held. Behind the huts were the farms, clearings hacked and burnt out of the forest and fenced off with thorn bushes. Had the travellers but known it, the forest was full of such clearings. The red earth was turned over, the yams, coco-yams and plantains grown for a few years till the soil was exhausted. Then another clearing would be made, the forest hacked down, the undergrowth burnt, and new plots planted. The old clearing would be left,

perhaps for centuries, to be covered again by the forest. At one time or another almost all the hundreds of square miles of dark, hostile-looking forest had been cleared in this way.

It was a market day at one of the villages on the road and the travellers found themselves accompanied by men and women filing onto the pathway along tiny tracks from all over the forest. They carried on their heads trays of yams (huge earthy potatoes with a coarse grey skin – you can see these in the picture on page 17), bunches of plantains (a sort of banana) with skins still green or brown, and all sorts of vegetables: tiny green and red peppers, squashes, pumpkins, bitter leaf (which looks like spinach), coco-yams (like new potatoes in appearance), and okra (a tiny, dark green tapering vegetable with little pips inside, like a small marrow coming out of the flower stage).

A bunch of palm nuts. The palm nut was one day to replace gold, ivory, cloth, and slaves as an object of trade. The kernels from these nuts were crushed to give a rich oil useful for cooking. The husks would make a lower grade oil. Today palm oil can be used to help make, among other things, soap, margarine and ice-cream.

Kola nuts offered for sale by a little Nigerian girl. Nuts like these, grown in the forests of Benin, may eventually have found their way along the caravan routes as far as Morocco, Tunis or Tripoli.

Sometimes there were bunches of orange-coloured palm kernels gathered from the palm trees that grew wild in the forest. In the pots which some of the women carried was the palm oil extracted from the crushed kernels; rich, brown, syrupy stuff, good and wholesome for cooking, and also used to rub on the body so that the skin remained soft and glistening. Other women carried the sap from the palm trees. This had been drained from cuts in the trunk right at the top of the tree by men who specialised in this dangerous job. Within a few hours it turned into palm wine. Within a few days it was very strong indeed. Some men carried on their heads trays of leathery kola nuts, about the size of a walnut. These split neatly into parts, and perhaps for this reason were a symbol of friendship, offered and shared wherever people met in West Africa. A few fishermen had come right up from the coast with loads of dried fish, brown and smelly, which they sold in the villages or in the town of Benin itself, for the Benin people were farmers and landsmen and knew little about fishing or the sea.

If you looked carefully in the market you might find other things; tiny deer, bush pigs, porcupine shot by the hunters in the forest, plump bush rats, and even the odd snails and tortoises picked up by the children. Altogether the people fed well, on mountains of yams boiled and pounded like mashed potatoes, or fried in palm oil; plantains and palm oil which were as good as meat for building their bodies; and quantities of green vegetables. They probably ate little meat

A village street near Benin.

You can buy almost anything in a West African market place. This old lady in modern Lagos is selling shells, okra, skulls (probably to make charms), pepper, coco-yams, firewood, dried fish, wild cat skins and pieces of cloth.

beyond what the hunters brought in. The goats, chicken, dogs, and the occasional skinny sheep that wandered about the villages were rarely killed at all except as sacrifices during religious ceremonies. Eggs and milk were almost unknown as food. It was a starchy diet. The children, in particular, who played stark naked in the streets till they were thirteen or fourteen, had tummies round as barrels from all the yams they ate. The men and women, though, were fairly tall and well-built, deep-chested, well-muscled, and very black.

Like the officials who had accompanied the travellers from the coast, the farmers wore kilts of cotton, usually dyed blue. In the fields they probably worked in just a loin cloth or a couple of bunches of leaves. In the town they might throw a kind of cloak across their shoulders.

The forests through which the travellers marched were full of people. Far back from their path the hunters and farmers were at work, and in the villages the way was thronged with men and women, buying and selling and bargaining. In the huts and booths about the market place the weavers, basket-makers, blacksmiths, doctors, potters, mat-makers and carpenters were at work, while the local nobility and the officials from Benin held court and settled arguments with the authority of the Oba. Benin was obviously a wealthy kingdom.

3. Great Benin

Even in the depths of the forest there was evidence of the Oba's power. The Oba's men went with the travellers. It would have been death for anyone to touch them or their belongings. At each nightly stop villagers could be turned out of their houses to give the Portuguese shelter. Away from the villages, by the side of the path, they sometimes passed pots of water and, beside them, shells. These had been placed there at the Oba's command for the benefit of travellers, who could help themselves to the water, using the shells to drink with. After

three or four days' march, the travellers approached the city of Benin itself. The farms were close together for the last two or three miles of their journey. Ditches and banks of earth which surrounded some of them connected with each other and wandered nearly a hundred miles through the undergrowth. These marked off the villages and farms which came under the direct control of Benin city itself.

At last they came to the city of Benin. At the end of the day they stood beneath the great inner wall, a huge mound of earth, as high and as wide as a two-storey house, six miles long, surrounding the most important part of Benin. Outside this was a ditch as deep and as wide as the wall was high and thick, and already beginning to be choked with thorn bushes. Both the wall and the ditch were still quite new when the Portuguese first came. Benin was at war, and might have to stand siege. At the Oba's command 5000 men must have worked for a whole dry season, five months, to pile up forty-eight million cubic feet of earth into the rampart. A massive fortified earthwork entrance guarded the travellers' way in. It was supported by timber, and watched by soldiers with swords slung under their left armpits. A heavy wooden door closed the gate. Normally a traveller bringing goods into the city would have to pay a toll before the gate was opened, but this time, at a word from the official with the white staff, the great door swung back. The first Europeans entered Benin.

Ahead of them as far as they could see, ran a long earthen street, forty yards wide, full of people, and among them the occasional goat or hen. About a mile ahead they noticed a huge tree standing by itself, and beyond that the road still ran into the distance. To the right were high earthen walls, a dull red colour, carefully smoothed into a series of horizontal ripples. The tops of these walls were thatched to prevent them being washed away by the rain. A great thatched gate could be seen, guarded by more soldiers, and beyond this was a glimpse of steeply sloping roofs and pointed towers. At the top of each of these the evening sunlight gleamed on bronze eagles. This was the Oba's palace.

To the left of the main highway was the rest of the city. It was perhaps a mile across and larger than most European towns at that time. From the main highway ran a number of broad streets, dividing the city into quarters or wards. The streets were clean and free from rubbish; the ward chiefs were responsible for that to the Oba. Each householder was expected to keep his section of the street clean, and the red mud surface of his house walls neat and polished till, as one European was to say, it shone like a looking glass.

The houses were built very close together, and it was to one of these that the travellers were taken for the night. The red thatched walls were lower than those of the palace. Only the Oba was allowed to build as high as seven eighteen-inch courses of mud block, and only very important nobles could build up to four or five courses. Within their walls were a

The wall of a house in modern Benin. A mud wall like this would soon wash away in the rains, so the top has to be protected. This used to be done with a thatch of grass or leaves but nowadays corrugated iron is used — less beautiful but more efficient. The drawing on the opposite page shows a gate in the city wall as it might have been when the Portuguese arrived. This wall is much bigger than a house wall but you can see how it was roofed over too.

15

series of small courtyards. There were dozens of these, for several hundred people, wives, children, relatives, visitors and servants might live in the house of a powerful nobleman. The larger part of every Benin house was open to the rain, which fell heavily into an open space dug at the centre of each courtyard, and then drained away under the house through a pipe made of a hollow palm trunk. Around each court were galleries, each about three feet wide. The roofs above the galleries were supported by light timbering, and were made of a heavy thatch of leaves. The appearance of each courtyard was oddly like that of a Roman house, and it was at once living room, bedroom, dining room and chapel.

In one of the four galleries was always a shrine, a platform of mud, and on it a variety of objects of clay, wood, bone, stone, or, if the family was particularly important, of bronze or ivory. There would be little statuettes in human form, carvings of animals, birds, or snakes, and perhaps one or two ancient stone axe-heads which were often found on the farms. These were believed to be thunderbolts left there by lightning. All sorts of different gods or beliefs could have their shrines, and ceremonies were held daily, monthly and annually by different members of the household. The traces of these ceremonies, the feathers of cockerels, the blood of dogs or goats, the remains of palm wine or food, usually lay about the shrines. The world of the gods and spirits was as real to the people of Benin as the everyday world of farms and houses and human beings.

In one of the other galleries the visitors were brought water, and were allowed to wash, change and rest. Then food was brought to them – a wooden platter of pounded yam, and pots of highly spiced soup or sauce containing palm oil, peppers, and perhaps a little meat or fish. Seated round the mound of yam, the Portuguese were expected to take lumps of yam with their fingers, dip them in the sauce or stew, and eat. The meal was washed down with calabashes of palm wine. It was a heavy meal. Their sleeping mats were laid out in another gallery, on the floor, or on an earthen bench against the wall. The visitors lay down and covered themselves with a cloth. Outside the streets were quiet except for the far-off barking of a dog, but everywhere in the tropical night the warm air was full of the sound of insects, crickets, moths, beetles and mosquitoes, buzzing, humming and whining in their ears as they fell asleep.

Sorting yams, the staple food of the people of Benin. The women will first boil the big tubers and then pound them with long poles. The pulp can then be cooked in various ways: as cakes fried in oil, or as a kind of dumpling served with soup.

In the two pictures below you can see how the pots are made. This potter is beginning by smoothing her clay over an up-ended old pot which served as a mould. She makes a basin-like shape, taking great care to keep it an equal thickness all over. Then she turns it the right way up and mitres on to it as many strips of clay as she needs to make it the required size. She will shape its neck and finish it with a rim.

In the next picture, a framework of boughs can be seen on which the pots to be fired have been arranged in rows and packed tight. Thick layers of fuel, either more branches, or grass or bamboo leaves, will be put on top of them and pressed down until there are no gaps to allow draughts of cold air to get in to the pots. The heap is set alight in several places and develops a great heat inside. After two hours, the pots are baked enough and they are uncovered.

4. The palace

The travellers woke early. The air was damp on their cheeks. A heavy mist had soaked their coverings and clung to the walls of the courtyard. Somewhere in the house a cock crew, and in the kitchens beyond the courtyard there was a steady thumping noise as a woman pounded yams with a heavy wooden pestle in a wooden mortar. Through the northern gates of the city women were already carrying their water pots on their heads down the narrow paths worn deep in the soft sandstone, to the Ikpoka brook. By the time the Portuguese had eaten their breakfast, probably a few fried plantains and some palm wine, the town was about its business. One of the two city markets might be in action, for they were held every fourth day. The farmers and hunters were in from the forest and the potters from just outside the city walls. White-gowned traders had brought trinkets and cloth down the trade paths from the merchant cities far north of Benin, which had received these goods from the camel caravans coming across the Sahara from the Mediterranean coast. Other traders had come by the same path as the Portuguese from the coast. The craftsmen of Benin city itself were squatting about the market with their own goods for sale.

As the travellers wandered about the markets and the streets, never left by the officials who had come up with them from the coast, they soon found that each craft had its own section of the town – all the leather workers in one group of buildings, all the weavers in another, the drum-makers in another, the brass-smiths and ivory carvers in others, and so on. There were forty such quarters in the town, each with its own trade association, with its chiefs and lesser ranks.

Always the travellers found that the centre of Benin life was the Oba's palace. Many of the craftsmen, such as the bronze-casters or the carvers of wood or ivory, could only be employed by the Oba himself. Trade with people from outside Benin only went on with the Oba's permission and under the control of his officials. The most valuable of all

Groundnuts and spices for sale.

19

the goods belonged to the king entirely: most of the ivory, all slaves, all leopard skins, all pepper, all palm kernels and all coral were the Oba's alone. However important the trade guilds and their heads may have been, or the nineteen town chiefs who had their palaces just outside the walls, it was the Oba who controlled the kingdom.

Later next day the Portuguese were escorted into the palace itself. It was enormous, as large as a small European town. Not only was it the Oba's dwelling place, it was the centre of government, a military headquarters and barracks, and a cathedral. According to one visitor you had to pass through four separate gates, each with a great empty space in front of it, before you came to the centre where the Oba himself lived. It is probable that not even he knew how many court-yards were in the palace, or how many people lived there.

There were, to begin with, three separate sections of the palace, in each of which lived an association of men and their families and servants whose duty and honour it was to serve the Oba. In one part were those who looked after the Oba's wardrobe, his clothes, his regalia and his ornaments. In another were those who looked after his wives and children. In the third section lived the Oba himself, surrounded by those who were his personal servants, preparing his food and looking after his comfort.

Each of these parts of the palace was jealously guarded. Sentries were placed to prevent any of the Oba's servants moving into a part of the palace that did not belong to his association.

As they passed through the series of heavily guarded gates the visitors realised that everywhere there were shrines, just as there had been in the houses on the other side of the town. Each shrine had its own courtyard and in some way or other each was dedicated to the Oba. Some were to worship the Oba's ancestors. Heads to represent them had been cast in bronze, so delicately that they were almost egg-shell thin.

The Altar of the King's Hand (bronze, 18 in (46 cm) high, made in the eighteenth century). A man's hand signified his power to do things and achieve success, particularly in war. So there were special ceremonies to honour the Oba's hand. You can also see here the leopards, another symbol of strength.

left: Bronze head of a queen mother. This beautiful head was probably made in the second quarter of the sixteenth century. It is 20 in (51 cm) high. The Oba's mother was allowed a particularly important place in the kingdom, with her own palace and special privileges. The male head on the right is later, dating from the seventeenth century – height $11\frac{3}{4}$ in (30 cm).

right: A bronze plaque from a pillar in one of the palace courts. There were about a thousand such plaques. This one is $22\frac{1}{2}$ in (57 cm) high and shows carved pillars supporting the shingled roof. Down the roof twists the image of a great snake, while two soldiers and two boys stand on either side of a palace shrine.

opposite: The Oba still has his shrines at the centre of the Benin palace. As well as his own shrine, he has shrines to his father and grandfather. In this picture you can see the mud walls of a palace court. On the mud platforms of the shrines are bronze statues and bells. Carved ivory tusks are supported by elaborate bronze heads. On the centre shrine you can see the lattice-like carving of the ebere, the ceremonial sword.

As well as bronze heads there were little bronze figures of the Oba himself in full regalia, escorted by his attendants, or by members of his court, or of sacred beasts such as the leopard; bronze bells and clappers, sacred utensils, sacrificial swords, spears, clubs and wands of office lay on the altars; huge elephant tusks leaned with the points towards the wall, carved from end to end with human and animal figures. As well as these altars to the dead there were others devoted to the welfare of the living Oba. Every part of his body had its own ritual and its own altar to safeguard the Oba's powers. Only if the Oba was healthy was the kingdom safe.

On either side of the last set of gates was a long gallery, supported by wooden pillars carved into the shape of merchants, soldiers and hunters. Through these last gates the Portuguese came into the central building. Here the Oba lived. They had seen the pointed towers with their bronze eagles long before. From the pinnacle of the central tower sixty feet above the ground a great copper snake curved downwards, its head poised above the central shingled porch. On the walls and on the heavy pillars that supported the galleries were the bronze plaques on which the smiths of Benin recorded events in the history of the kingdom. On these plaques soldiers were shown

leading their captives home, Obas receiving ambassadors, noblemen taking part in processions. One day the Portuguese themselves would be depicted in their national dress, with their swords, their armour and their guns. This was one way in which a people who did not have the skills of reading and writing could keep a record of their past.

Everywhere through this central part of the palace was bronze and ivory. A whole industry of bronze workers and ivory carvers depended on the worship of the Oba. For centuries these craftsmen were allowed to work for no-one else. In that time they built up in the Oba's palace perhaps the most marvellous collection of art and craftsmanship in Africa. These men, some of them geniuses, were but part of the enormous number of people whose whole time was devoted to the worship of the Oba. They included the leopard-keepers, the elephant hunters and the fish-eagle hunters. There were ten noblemen who looked after the royal wardrobe, nine who controlled his servants, and twelve who guarded the harem. There were the sixty titleholders from the palace associations who had a place in one of the annual religious ceremonies. There were hundreds of lesser officials. Indeed every man in the kingdom had some part to play in the worship of the Oba. As his subjects, all could claim membership of one of the palace associations if they could pay the initiation fee. They could then enter the palace and devote their lives to the service of the Oba, in the hope that one day they might be promoted to one of the leading positions in the palace associations. The Oba, in his palace, was the centre of the kingdom.

The Oba rides in procession supported on either side by noblemen. The man on the Oba's right carries the standard called the Bird of Disaster. You can read about this on page 41.

right: A Portuguese soldier and his dog go hunting. This plaque, 14½ in (37 cm) high, is one of several which show the Portuguese hunting leopard.

5. The king who was God

The Oba himself was the most powerful of the Benin gods. There were other gods who had to be pleased: Osa, the creator; his son Oloku who was at once god of river and of sea, and of childbirth; Ogun, god of iron, hunters and war; Osu, god of medicine. There were cults, such as the Ifa cult, whose priests told the future by throwing a string of beads on the ground and looking at the pattern in which it fell. There was an army of spirits, for the dead had to be pleased, lest they should come back and bring evil to the family. There were doctors who could bring disease or cure it, or could fly, or turn into animals, or disappear. There were witches who killed secretly, drawing the life slowly out of their victims. They came from all over West Africa to meet, particularly around certain trees. Their lights could be seen glowing after dark, during the hot thundery weather that comes at the beginning and the end of the rainy season.

Terrible as all these were, it was the Oba who had to be worshipped above all. Probably no ruler in Africa was held in quite so much dread as the Oba of Benin at that time. On his health depended the welfare of the crops and the victories of his armies. He came out of his palace only to make war or to be worshipped. At intervals throughout the year the Oba took part in religious ceremonies. When the new yams were dug up in November, it was the Oba who safeguarded them at a ceremony at the palace. There was another rite to make sure the soil remained fertile, another to cleanse the city of evil, another held in the palace when the Oba's regalia was sprinkled with human blood, others which safeguarded the various parts of the king's body. Above all there was the great ceremony of the king's head, when the king appeared in the city before the whole nation.

Through the great thatched gates came the king's attendants, servants and guards, and the king's hunters who led live leopards, chained by the neck, grunting menacingly. Then came the musicians: drummers, men beating gongs, blowing horns, trumpets, flutes and fifes, shaking calabashes and clanging bells. All the great officials rode on horseback: the seven uzama (members of the Oba's council), the nineteen Eghaevo N'Ogbe (the town chiefs), all the Exaevo (noblemen who had a part to play in the worship of the Oba). All these wore the coral necklaces awarded by the Oba, and anklets, bangles and rings of bronze and ivory made by the Oba's craftsmen.

The Oba as a god. The maker of this bronze plaque shows him as being far more than human as he swings two leopards by their tails. His feet are shown as the heads of two cat-fish – one of the legends about an early Oba.

Then came the Oba himself, on foot, dressed from head to waist in red coral. On his head was a pointed crown of coral, with a fringe of coral beads over his forehead; coral necklaces were loaded around his throat from chin to shoulders; over his body was a massive shirt of coral beads; from his waist he was swathed in cotton skirts that hid his legs and feet (there was a belief among some of his subjects that an earlier Oba had fish instead of feet, as you can see from the picture on page 26); from his hips hung pendants of bronze and carved ivory; on his wrists were bangles of ivory and bronze. Each arm was supported by a nobleman of the palace, naked to the waist. Two others, also bare to the waist, held scarlet fans above his head to protect him from the sun. With him walked two young men, naked except for a bronze anklet, who carried the execution swords, the cruel wide-bladed ada and the ceremonial eben execution knives, upright before them; with these walked young boys carrying the strange brass ebere, which looked like huge spear blades; behind them came the executioner, the Isiemwero, with his wicked spiked club. Around them all leapt and tumbled the dwarves and deaf-mutes the Oba kept for his amusement.

above left: Akenzua II, the present Oba of Benin (1972) in his regalia. You will notice that almost everything he wears is shown on the ancient bronzes of Obas: the coral headdress, necklaces and shirt, and the ivory ornaments at his waist and on his wrist.

An ivory waist mask (9¾ in (25 cm) high) made for an Oba during the sixteenth century. The Portuguese were probably still frequent visitors at court, hence the carvings of Portuguese heads around the top.

overleaf: The Oba and some of his attendants. A modern artist's idea of the procession.

27

Behind the Oba came his women, 600 of them according to one European. Their hair had been shaved in complicated patterns, plaited and greased for months beforehand, with extra hair-pieces and coral beads worked into it. Their faces were made up with patterns of white and coloured clay. They wore necklaces of coral, armlets and anklets of copper and iron, and their fingers were loaded with copper rings. They were clothed from shoulder to toe in fine cotton cloth elaborately patterned in bright colours. Then came the soldiers. Their commanders were on horse-back, wrapped in scarlet cloaks, wearing necklaces of leopard and elephant teeth, and with horsetails dangling from behind their red, fur-trimmed caps. On each side of them strode attendants with great fans to shield their heads from the sun. The cavalrymen armed with spears and swords sat on the backs of mules. Behind them strode the infantrymen, bare-chested, with their swords, spears, shields and bows.

With the soldiers came the victims for sacrifice, probably from the prison, arms tied behind their backs, mouths tightly gagged. The number of these varied. When the Portuguese first arrived only a few may have been sacrificed

In Benin today the religious rites still take place. Here the Oba is returning to his throne in a pavilion and pauses as he holds up his ceremonial sword.

top left: A very old member of the Oba's family. She is a princess in her own right and has permission to wear coral. She is wearing a very high horsehair wig, studded all over with coral and ivory ornaments. On her face are painted traditional tribal marks. With other members of the royal family, she is watching the festival.

The festival includes a ceremony in which the town is finally cleansed of any evil spirits that remain after all the previous sessions of worship have been concluded. The Oba dances to the drums with his chiefs. It is difficult for him to do so as his costume is extremely heavy.

During the ceremony, all the chiefs dance up to salute the Oba, beginning with the lowest in rank. They toss their ornamental swords into the air, catch them again and give him a special greeting. They are splendidly dressed. Here are two chiefs dancing and saluting the Oba.

at these ceremonies, but later it is said that hundreds died.

The Benin people saw nothing horrible in this. They, like the Portuguese who visited them, were used to death. Over half their children died before they were five, as did children in Europe at this time. Disease, famine, accident and warfare were as familiar to them as they were to the Europeans. The spirits of the dead were never far away. A death, however violent, which enabled the Oba to safeguard their kingdom was a good death. A man sent to serve his master in such a way could be sure of a high place in the world of the spirits. Many of the palace noblemen understood that part of their responsibility was to accept death when the Oba, their master, died. The Portuguese were often to be astonished by the confidence and pride with which the victims went to their execution.

This was never more astonishing than when the Oba died. Of course, as he was more than human, he was never said to have died, as he could never be said to sleep, eat, or wash. He was simply going to take up his court in another world. There were two funerals. Both were held within the Oba's palace. For the first funeral a deep hole was dug, wider at the bottom than at the top. The king's corpse was seated on a throne and placed at the bottom, attended by his servants and several of the titled men of Benin. The grave was closed, and the men left with their master. Each day the grave was opened, to ask who had been the first to join the Oba, and therefore the first to attend the Oba in the next world. After four or five days there was no further answer from the darkness. All had willingly gone to their deaths with their king. Over the tomb a great fire was heaped up. A feast of sacrificial meat was made, and through the streets of Benin went masked men with drawn swords, cutting down all whom they met. A few days later there would be a second funeral, and around the Oba's body would be placed his clothes, his regalia, and his wealth. For centuries, all over West Africa, ceremonies like this had taken place, the king laid in state to rest with his belongings and servants about him, taking them with him to another world.

The group of three figures is cast in bronze and stands in the centre of the altar sacred to Eweka II, the father of the present Oba of Benin. The figure on the throne is a portrait of the late king. Behind the centrepiece are some tall, carved ebony sticks, each of which represents one of the king's ancestors.

6. Prester John

A seventeenth-century engraving of Sao Jorge da Mina, the Portuguese headquarters in West Africa founded in 1482. From here and other forts on the coast of what is now Ghana, Portuguese ships sailed to Benin during the sixteenth century. Later they sailed from the island of Sao Tome, and the Dutch occupied Elmina as the fort came to be called.

De Sequira returned to Portugal and described what he had seen. Over the next few years the Portuguese came to know the coast of Africa quite well. Their ships entered almost all the creeks that wound through the mangrove swamps of the Niger delta. Further north they built a fort on the coast of modern Ghana, which still stands and is called Elmina – the mine. Slaves, palm oil, leopard skins and beads were brought back to it to be exchanged for the gold from the mines in the interior. Increasingly it was the interior of Africa with its wealth and its secrets which interested them.

In 1486 the Portuguese king sent Joao Affonso d'Aveiro to Benin. He was not, like de Sequira, just an adventurous sea captain in a small ship with a few ragged sailors, but a nobleman sent as an ambassador from one king to another. He came twice, and on his second visit was to die in Benin. The Benin court had taken little notice of de Sequira, but d'Aveiro's visits were remembered centuries later in the traditions of the royal court, and were commemorated on the bronze plaques that recorded important events in Benin history. The Oba and the king of Portugal exchanged letters. For the first time some of the secrets of Benin were revealed to Europeans.

D'Aveiro brought back a report which startled the Portuguese then, and has mystified historians ever since.

An elderly man had talked to the Portuguese of the death of the previous Oba. Far to the east, said the old man, was a great kingdom, older and greater than Benin. Its ruler was called the Ogane, he said. When the old Oba died his death had to be reported to the Ogane before the next Oba could reign. Once

Visitors to Benin.
far left: Mounted bronze figures, possibly representing envoys from the Muslim trading states north of the Sahara. The one on the left dates from about 1600. The other is later. Sizes 19 and $23\frac{1}{2}$ in high (48 and 60 cm).
left: A bronze statue, $22\frac{1}{2}$ in (57 cm) high, probably made in the late seventeenth century. Although the figure was made in Benin, the face marks show that it represents a Yoruba nobleman, possibly a messenger from Ife. He wears on his breast a cross like the one which so puzzled the Portuguese when they first saw it in Benin.

upon a time the Oba's body would have been taken to the Ogane's court for burial. It had been the custom, the old man said. He himself had been entrusted with the message and had travelled for twenty months, that is for twenty full changes of the moon before he reached the Ogane's court. So great a king was the Ogane that no human eye was ever allowed to see him. The old man described how he had been received by the Ogane from behind a screen, and how, at the very end of the audience he had been allowed a glimpse of the Ogane's foot. He told the Portuguese what he had brought back to Benin: a crown shaped rather like a helmet, a sceptre and one other object. He had himself been given a small replica of this last object. The old man showed it to the Portuguese. It was a cross.

The Portuguese were so amazed that they later arranged for the old man to go to Portugal with his cross. To them the cross meant Christianity. Was the Ogane a Christian? They remembered again the myth of Prester John, and began to wonder if at last they were about to find him. But the legend of Prester John, as they were one day to discover, referred to the ancient kingdom of Abyssinia far away on the other side of Africa. The Ogane was another person entirely.

We do not know, even now, who exactly the Ogane was, but we think he was the ruler of the city of Ife. Ife was the home of some of the greatest craftsmen and artists in African history. They made beautiful statues in bronze and clay that were not seen by Europeans till the end of the nineteenth century. Ife is 120 miles from Benin. It is probably the oldest and certainly the most sacred of the many towns and cities belonging to the Yoruba people who live in the south-western part of Nigeria. The Yoruba themselves describe how it was reached by the founder of their nation, Oduduwa, in flight from the Hausa cities to the north. This may have been 500 years before d'Aveiro reached Benin, and there were people living at Ife even then. It became mighty under Oduduwa, and from it went his sons who are said to have founded other great walled cities within the forest, including Benin.

It was one of the sons of Oduduwa who was believed to have become the first Oba of Benin. The Portuguese were probably told the story. Once upon a time, it was said, there were no kings of Benin. One day, however, there was an argument among the Edo, the tribe who lived in Benin, about who should rule them. Unable to settle the dispute they asked Oduduwa to

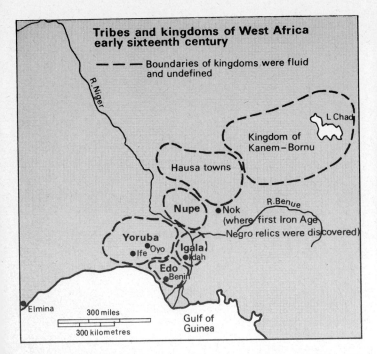

Tribes and kingdoms of West Africa early sixteenth century

Heads from Ife: these recently discovered heads are thought to be 600–700 years old. Though moulded not in metal but in terra-cotta, are these the forerunners of the Benin bronze sculptures? The Yoruba say that in the reign of Oba Ogunola in the thirteenth or fourteenth century, the bronze caster Igueghae was sent from Ife to teach the Benin people how to work in bronze. The bronze casters of Ife were some of the most skilled in the world. The earlier bronze heads from Benin (see page 21) look rather like those from Ife: life-like and simple in design. Later the Benin style changed as you can see from the pictures on page 46.

send one of his sons to look after them. He was too sensible to risk one of his sons, and sent instead seven lice to be guarded carefully and returned in three years time. The lice were carefully looked after in Benin in the hair of a slave, and returned at the end of the appointed time, fatter than before. Pleased that so much care should have been taken of such lowly creatures, Oduduwa sent his son, Oranmiyan to be the first Oba of Benin. He married an Edo princess, from whom all later Obas were descended, but then had so much trouble governing the Edo that he left the country for ever, calling it 'a land of vexation', and went away north to found the city of Oyo far off on the edge of the grasslands. This was how the Oba's courtiers explained the history of Benin, and everywhere the Portuguese went there was evidence of how much had been gained from Ife, that mysterious city no European was to visit until late in the nineteenth century. The religion and mystery that surrounded the Oba seem to have come from Ife. His enormous palace with its innumerable courts and shrines, its associations and ceremonies, was like other enormous and complicated palaces in Ife and other Yoruba towns. Some of the gods whom the Oba and his people worshipped were from Ife and the

35

Yoruba. The art of Benin, above all that of bronze work, is said to be from Ife. The descendants of the first Ife craftsman to come to Benin still lived in their own quarter of the city, and carried out their sacred skill. The blue beads, so much valued in Benin and everywhere else in West Africa may have been smelted in Ife.

The Portuguese were never to find out who the Ogane was, nor ever to visit Ife. The lands to the north remained closed to them. Although they met the occasional visitor from the north (like the ones in the picture on page 34), they never discovered who the mysterious strangers were.

We now know much more about Benin than the Portuguese did. European and Nigerian historians have been able to collect and write down the traditions of Benin and of the Yoruba that had once been handed down by word of mouth. Increasingly since the nineteen-forties the archaeologists have been able to dig up the evidence of a history far older than these traditions, and while much is still uncertain, some links have been discovered.

We know, for example, that there were other nations inland who worked in bronze like the Yoruba, and who, like the Yoruba, had some part to play in the history of Benin. The Igala, whose capital lies at Idah on the River Niger, had rulers who were still related to the Oba of Benin when d'Aveiro was visiting him. Further north up the River Niger were the Nupe, in whose territory can still be seen bronze figures very much like those of Benin and Ife. Related to both these were the Jukun, workers in bronze, and rulers of an empire that may once have extended from the Niger delta to the very edge of the Sahara desert.

Ife head, height 12¾ in (32.5 cm). What are the lines on the face? Were they perhaps made by the artist to reduce the reflection from the bronze surface? Do they represent strings of beads hanging from a crown? It is most likely that they show the pattern of scars cut on the wearer while he was still a baby. These were made with a tiny sliver of quartz or glass, and kept open with charcoal till the scars had been formed. This sort of operation is still carried out in the countryside in many parts of Africa, the pattern varying according to tribe and rank. Here you can also see holes on the upper lip and along the jaw. There may once have been hair inserted to make a beard and a moustache.

Further afield still and earlier than these, before the use of bronze reached the forests of southern Nigeria (brought possibly by immigrants from across the desert), the archaeologists have discovered an even older Negro culture. They call it the Nok culture after the village in the centre of Nigeria where its remains were first found. It is at least 2500 years old. Its people knew the use of iron and were particularly skilful at making statues of men and animals out of baked clay. Were these the forerunners of those who were later to model in bronze in Ife, Nupe, Idah and, last of all, Benin?

We have learnt a great deal about Benin, but there are still a lot of questions to be answered. Where did their worship of the king come from? The Yoruba and the Edo once liked to believe that it came from Egypt. Where did the strange architecture of the Benin houses come from? It was probably just a sensible way to build in a country without stone and where timber was destroyed by white ants. Even so, many travellers noted these buildings as just one example of a similarity between the customs and beliefs of West Africa and those of Roman or Carthaginian North Africa. Some of the gods and religious beliefs seem to have been very much the same in both parts of Africa.

The most puzzling question of all is still the one that faced the Portuguese. Who was the Ogane? It is thought that the Ogane and the ruler of Ife were the same person, but it is not certain. The Portuguese reported that the Ogane lived to the east of Benin. Ife is north west. It took the old man twenty months to reach him. It takes less than a fortnight to walk the distance between Ife and Benin.

The cross the old man brought back is still a mystery. We do not know whether it was used at Ife or not. It was sometimes used by priests and craftsmen who worked for the Nupe and for the Jukun. We would still like to know more about the history of Benin.

The Nok head (shown here at its actual size) is at least two thousand years old. The people who made this were among the first Negroes to smelt iron, south of the Sahara. The skill which they used to make these clay figures may eventually have been handed on to the bronze casters of Ife and Benin. This took place over a very long period, and we still have to learn how it happened.

This bronze figure has been seated at Tada on the River Niger, hundreds of miles from Ife or Benin, for at least five hundred years. It is 20 in (51 cm) high and only egg-shell thick. Both hands and one foot have been worn away where it has been polished with river sand. The same skill that was needed by the bronze casters of Ife and Benin was needed to make this masterpiece. No one is yet certain when, where, or by whom it was made.

7. A warrior kingdom

When d'Aveiro came the second time the war drums were thundering. It was the dry season, the time for war, when the crops had been gathered in, the young men were idle and movement was easy along the forest paths. The Oba Esigie, like his predecessors, was pushing out the frontiers of his kingdom in every direction. This time the enemy was the ruler of Idah, a member of the same family as the Oba.

War had come suddenly. The drums were echoing day and night through the city, and murmuring far off in the forest as the news spread and the forces of Benin were summoned. The court officials came and went with their white wands of office to send orders and bring back news. The city was full of rumours that Idah soldiers were moving on them from the north; that there was treachery in Benin itself; that the greatest of the palace nobles, the head of the Oba's council, had turned against the king. He was angry, it was said, because the Oba had proved his favourite wife to be unfaithful to him. There were stories of a plot to ambush and capture the Oba himself.

The day after the war had been announced the troops were pouring into the city from every village in the kingdom. Almost all of them were footsoldiers, young men straight from the farms, led by local chiefs or noblemen. Each man carried a large oblong shield, a basketwork affair woven from palm leaves or made of elephant hide, slung on his back with his spear, his bow and his arrows. Each carried a short broad-bladed sword slung under his arm, and a crude helmet made of leather or basketwork. They thronged the courtyards and galleries of the town's houses, wherever they had relatives. They slept in the streets. They drank, danced and rioted through the night. The markets were full of armourers; the smiths beat out swords and spear-heads; the priests prepared charms to protect the soldiers or brewed the venom that tipped

Benin soldier with elaborate head-dress, basket-work shield, leopard skin, and spear, prepares for war. He is attended by two Portuguese soldiers, and two musicians. One of the musicians blows a horn, another rattles a gourd. Bronze plaque, 17 in (43.2 cm) high.

the arrows. Market women sold pots of palm wine, and sat in front of the heaps of yams, plantains and fish that the soldiers would need to take with them.

Within a week Benin was ready. The secret part of the preparations was over, the sacrifices, human and animal, made within the palace walls. In the morning silence descended on the town. Then the drums and the gongs boomed, the flutes squealed, and the gates of the palace swung open. The Oba came out to wage war. Around him were his picked men, his personal bodyguard, the leaders of the palace associations, some on mules or horses and wrapped in their scarlet cloaks. Their spears made a forest about the king. The sun gleamed on leather helmets and black spear blades. At once the town was overwhelmed with noise, with the din of drums, of shouting and singing, of squealing fifes, of war cries and the whinnying of excited horses. The air was full of the smell of sweat and of choking red dust raised by thousands of stamping feet. The Oba and his commanders led the cavalcade along the main thoroughfare and out through the northern gate. From every ward of the city and out of every building surged the rest of the army, perspiring and jostling their way to the northern gates. To European onlookers they looked more like a migration than an army. There could have been 20,000 men marching out of the city, or there could have been 100,000. The Oba himself can never have known how many men served in his army. Hour after hour they trampled through the gates, splashed across the Ikpoba stream, and disappeared into the forest. Miles away to the north the distant sound of horns and drums showed where the head of the army filed along the pathway toward Idah. It was evening before the last soldiers cleared the northern gate and the wooden door creaked shut. Silence and darkness came upon the town. Apart from the handful of sentries on the gates there was not a young man to be found in Benin. In the markets the women quietly packed away what was left of their wares. The old men talked quietly to each other in the courtyards. The city waited.

A few weeks later a command came for the Portuguese ambassadors to go up to the battle front. They became the only Europeans to see a Benin army in action.

For several days they followed the pathway northward. It was soon clear how the war had affected the lives of the people along the path. The villages were deserted. The Oba's troops carried few provisions with them, and looted what they could

The Bird of Disaster, 13¼ in (33.8 cm) high, made in the eighteenth or nineteenth century

This is the bronze head of a battle standard. The bird is probably an ibis or a hornbill. The story goes that as the Oba Esigie passed through the gates of Benin on his way to fight the Ata of Idah in 1515 this bird of evil omen made discouraging sounds overhead. The Oba ordered the bird to be killed, and then went on to win the battle. After this, figures of the bird were cast in bronze and flogged during certain court ceremonies, to remind it that the Oba was not subject to the fate of ordinary men.

Two men play drums. A third is needed to support the biggest drum. The plaque on the right shows a musician plucking a tiny harp.

left: Benin warriors in action against an Ibo soldier. The Ibo, who has a characteristic pattern of scars or his face and wears a helmet of different style, has received a deep diagonal wound across his chest. This plaque is $15\frac{3}{4}$ in (40 cm) high.

find, wherever they could find it. The villagers had fled into the forest the moment they had heard the ominous sound of the drums and the flutes. Nearer to the front itself there was more evidence of the war. The little villages were blackened by fire, the huts and granaries charred and broken down. In one empty market place a man had been tied to a tree trunk. He had died several days before. Occasionally messengers on their way back to Benin would pass the Portuguese. They reported that the Oba had still to meet the Idah army in battle, and that the queen mother was marching with an army to support the Benin troops. One evening the travellers heard the noise of drums and shouting very low and far off to the north. The soldiers in their bodyguard did not sleep that night, but stood or sat with their weapons in their hands. No fire was lit. They said there had been a battle. As the light filtered down through the trees early the following morning an officer trotted into the camp. His red cloak was torn, and he looked exhausted, but his eyes glistened in his dust-covered face. He spoke a few words to the soldiers and disappeared southwards. He carried news of a victory. The queen mother's troops had surprised the Idah army and wiped it out.

That morning as they marched north the news was confirmed by trains of weary prisoners on their way south. They had been stripped of their arms, in some cases of their clothes, and their wrists were tied behind them. Roped together they trudged silently with bowed heads. They knew what waited for them in Benin. Their guards shouted jubilantly at the Portuguese envoys' bodyguard, sometimes showing a battered helmet or blunted sword as evidence of their prowess.

Nearer the battle there was even grimmer evidence of violence. Wounded men sat or lay moaning by the side of the path. Their wounds had sometimes been dressed with strips of cotton, but there was little other help to be given. Their wounds were already septic, and all but the most lightly injured would probably die.

The forest opened out and they came quite suddenly on the battlefield. The grass, once waist high had been trampled flat, and amongst it lay the dead. Benin soldiers were moving among them collecting weapons, shields and armour. A group of officers met the travellers and took them across the battle area, talking excitedly. The Idah army had been ambushed by the queen mother's army as it came out of the forest. At the

centre of the clearing the fighting had been bitter, and here the corpses lay close to each other.

In the centre of the carnage lay a dead horse. It had once carried the Idah general. The queen mother's head slave, who had led the Benin attack, had cut down the rider, and then been kicked to death himself by the terrified animal. The visitors were glad to leave the horrid place. The sun was high and the battlefield stank. Above the dead, who would be left where they lay, the vultures circled or perched, hunched hideously, in the trees round about. Away in the forest was heard the occasional distant shout. The last of the Idah army was being hunted down. It had been a complete victory.

That evening the Oba entertained the Portuguese. Delighted by the victory, he received them well. They ate that night with his son, and the stories of the battle were exchanged, to be recalled and remembered for centuries as part of the history of Benin. A few miles further on, had the Portuguese known it, flowed the River Niger past the city of Idah. It was nearly a mile wide, and had flowed nearly 2000 miles through West Africa before losing itself in the delta as it flowed out to sea. The Portuguese never saw the river. For 300 years the very existence of the mighty Niger was to be doubted by the Europeans.

The threat of invasion was over, but the campaign was not finished. The Oba withdrew his army to the edge of his own territory and there set up a war camp. For the rest of that year the Benin army lived within its defences and ravaged the country round about. The wretched farmers from the nearby villages, their own homes destroyed, were forced to build huts and farm for their conquerors. Their granaries were broken open to feed the soldiers. Their wives and daughters became the property of the Benin troops. They cooked for them and became their slaves. The land round about was cleared at the Oba's command and fields were planted. On some campaigns part of the army might expect to stay in such a camp for two or three years. It might then become a permanent settlement inhabited by Benin soldiers who had married local women, and who would use it as a base for further raids. This time, however, at the end of a year the Oba was wanted back in Benin for one of the great religious ceremonies without which the kingdom could not survive. He decided to abandon the camp and the army filed southward through the forest back to Benin. Another Benin war was over.

One of the reasons why the Oba was so interested in encouraging the Portuguese had been that he was expanding his empire. He wanted to use Portuguese weapons, for their firearms fascinated him and his people. Among the records they kept of the Portuguese are many which show them in their armour and with their guns. So far battles in the forest had been mainly hand to hand affairs, settled by spear and sword. With gunpowder and guns the Oba's armies would be able to blast their way from end to end of the forest. The Oba had welcomed the Portuguese envoys to obtain guns, as well as to learn about Europe and European religion. He traded with them, sent his son to be educated in Portugal, and even allowed Portuguese friars to preach Christianity in his kingdom, build churches and baptise hundreds of converts.

Portuguese soldiers. Although the bronze statuette was made about 1750 it is probably a copy of an earlier figure made to commemorate the help given by the Portuguese to the Oba Esigie in his campaign against the Ata of Idah. This figure is 17 in (43 cm) high and the plaque on the left is 19 in (48 cm) high.

8. Four centuries go by

The Portuguese had seen an African kingdom rising to the height of its power. By the end of the seventeenth century Benin controlled the whole of the coastline of modern Nigeria from Lagos in the west, which began as a war camp set up by Esigie's son, to Calabar in the east. Inland the Benin armies helped to found the great trading city of Onitsha on the Niger, and were claimed as founders by many Ibo clans in eastern Nigeria.

By this time, however, the Portuguese were coming less often to Benin. After Vasco da Gama opened the trade routes by sea with India in 1497 the price of the long-tailed Benin pepper fell. The warehouse which the Portuguese had built on the Benin River was closed. The friars were disappointed to find that their converts were just as unwilling to give up their old gods as they had been willing to accept the god of Christianity. They, too, left.

Nevertheless, Portuguese, and later English and Dutch ships continue to come each year to the Benin River. They brought the brightly coloured cloth – silver, red, gold – that was so popular in Benin, the fine cottons and linens, the glass-ware, the coral, the brass bracelets or 'manillas' that could be used as money or be melted down by the Oba's brass-smiths, iron bars, mirrors, glass beads and cowrie shells that were accepted as money in market places throughout West Africa. In return the Europeans bought cotton cloth which could be sold almost anywhere along the coast. Most of the cloth, dyed and patterned blue, was woven in Benin, though some came from still further inland. There was a profitable trade in the ivory won by the Oba's elephant hunters, in pepper when its price started to rise again in the seventeenth century, and in the blue 'coris' beads which were said to have been dug out of old graves in the

Bronze heads from the last days of the Benin empire. Much more copper could be gained from trade, and much of this was used to make the heads more and more massive in order to support an elephant tusk which came up through the top of the head. The head rests on a metal flange. The bead necklace rises up to the mouth, and the headdress becomes more and more complicated. The head on the right was made about 1890. Heights $20\frac{1}{2}$ and $21\frac{1}{4}$ in (52 and 54 cm). Compare these with the earlier heads on page 21.

interior. A few slaves were sold to the Europeans, but not many, for the Oba refused to allow male slaves to be sent out of his country.

Although Benin's trade was a prosperous one, the kingdom had little to do with the world outside Africa. In 400 years after d'Aveiro's visit hardly any Europeans ever reached the city of Benin itself. Only rumours of its affairs reached the coast. At the end of the seventeenth century its expansion seems to have come to an end. A series of civil wars was fought over the succession to the throne. The town chiefs rebelled against the

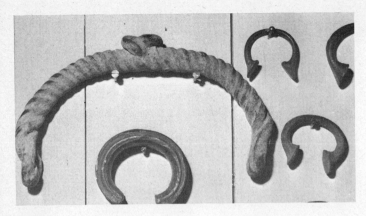

Manillas. These were pieces of copper or brass, sometimes made of twisted wire. You can see two Portuguese holding manillas if you look at page 43. Manillas were used as money all over West Africa for at least three hundred years, and were still being used in this way in some places in the mid-twentieth century.

Ivory salt cellar. This was ordered from a Benin craftsman by a wealthy Portuguese in the sixteenth century. The Portuguese noblemen on the salt cellar — there is another on the other side — both wear the cross of the Military Order of Christ. A man with a spyglass looks out from the crow's nest of the ship on top of the salt bowl; $11\frac{3}{4}$ in (30 cm) high.

Oba, and much of the city was abandoned. In the eighteenth and nineteenth centuries the Obas seemed to have regained their power once more.

Contact with the Europeans mattered very little to Benin. There were a few changes. The Oba's officials on the coast spoke Portuguese to visiting traders, and were known by the Portuguese title 'fiadors'. Benin farmers had orange and lemon trees on their farms, grew another root crop, cassava, which could be cooked and pounded like yam, and planted maize in their fields. All these had been brought by the Portuguese from the Mediterranean and from South America. The Benin army went into battle with muskets, which they fired from the hip, as they were likely to explode. Many of these had been made by Benin blacksmiths and those supplied by European traders were of poor quality. The Oba even possessed half a dozen of his own cannon.

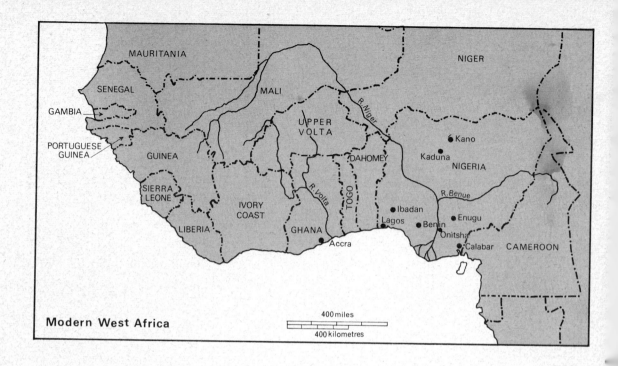

Modern West Africa

400 miles
400 kilometres

These changes did not amount to much. Benin in 1890 was still much the same as it had been in 1472. The Oba still reigned and was worshipped. The brass workers, ivory carvers and wood carvers still carried out their ancient crafts. The armies still marched into the forest every dry season. The great ceremonies were still carried out. The sacrifices were still made. But the outside world would be ignored no longer. In 1891 when the victim knelt before the executioner at the annual consecration of the royal regalia he shouted as the sword fell: 'The white men who are greater than you or I are coming shortly to fight and conquer you.' Greater? No. More powerful? Certainly. Six years later British soldiers and sailors, armed with guns, marched into Benin. It had become part of the modern world.

Street scene, Benin city, 1972.